EXPANDED EDITION

Grade 2

The *Seeds on the Move* lesson is part of the

Picture-Perfect STEM program K–2 written by the

program authors and includes lessons from their

award-winning series.

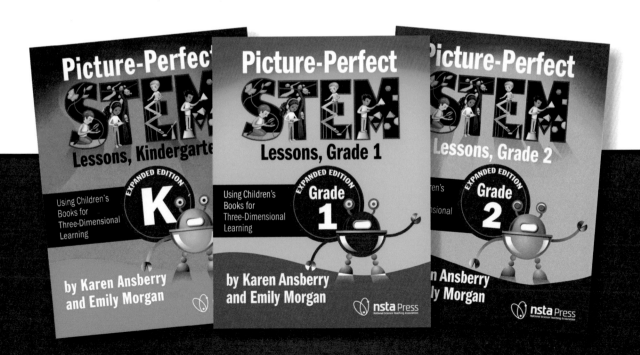

Seeds on the Move

Description

After observing the phenomenon of dandelion seeds being blown away by the wind, students investigate the various ways other plants disperse their seeds. They read about how wind and water help spread seeds, and they learn that some animals can even "plant" trees. Students take a "sock walk" in which they model one way that plants use animals to move their seeds around. Then they develop their own model that mimics an animal dispersing seeds.

Alignment with the *Next Generation Science Standards*

Performance Expectation		
2-LS2-2: Develop a simple model that mimics the function of an animal in dispersing seeds or pollinating plants.		
Science and Engineering Practice	**Disciplinary Core Ideas**	**Crosscutting Concept**
Developing and Using Models Develop a simple model based on evidence to represent a proposed object or tool.	**LS2.A: Interdependent Relationships in Ecosystems** Plants depend on animals for pollination or to move their seeds around. **ETS1.B: Developing Possible Solutions** Designs can be conveyed through sketches, drawings, or physical models. These representations are useful in communicating ideas for a problem's solutions to other people.	**Structure and Function** The shape and stability of structures of natural and designed objects are related to their functions.

Note: The activities in this lesson will help students move toward the performance expectations listed, which is the goal after multiple activities. However, the activities will not by themselves be sufficient to reach the performance expectations.

Featured Picture Books

TITLE: ***Flip, Float, Fly: Seeds on the Move***
AUTHOR: **JoAnn Early Macken**
ILLUSTRATOR: **Pam Paparone**
PUBLISHER: **Holiday House**
YEAR: **2016**
GENRE: **Non-Narrative Information**
SUMMARY: *Colorful paintings and simple text explain many different methods of seed dispersal. The end matter includes information on plant parts and explains that not all seeds sprout.*

TITLE: ***Who Will Plant a Tree?***
AUTHOR: **Jerry Pallotta**
ILLUSTRATOR: **Tom Leonard**
PUBLISHER: **Sleeping Bear Press**
YEAR: **2010**
GENRE: **Narrative Information**
SUMMARY: *This engaging and informative book depicts the ways seeds are dispersed by various animals' behaviors and body structures.*

Time Needed

This lesson will take several class periods. Suggested scheduling is as follows:

Session 1: **Engage** with Dandelion Observations and Wonderings

Session 2: **Explore** with Seed Observations and **Explain** with *Flip, Float, Fly* Read-Aloud

Session 3: **Explain** with Seeds on the Move Lift-the-Flap Booklet

Session 4: **Elaborate** with *Who Will Plant a Tree?* Read-Aloud and Sock Walk

Session 5: **Evaluate** with *Who Will Plant a Tree?* Model

Materials

Note: Dandelions bloom in the spring and fall but most abundantly in the spring. If the season or location is not right for finding dandelions, you can use the videos and photographs in the "Websites" section.

For Dandelion Observations and Wonderings (per student)

- Dandelions (including buds, flowers, and seed heads)

For Seed Observations (per group of four students)

- Collection of seeds featured in the book *Flip, Float, Fly*, such as dandelion, maple, locust, coconut, acorn, burdock (burr), or whole fig cut in half to reveal the seeds (Optional: Use seed cards.)
- Hand lenses

For Sock Walk (per student)

- Adult-size white or light-colored sock
- Hand lens
- (Optional) Gallon-size zippered plastic bag

For Seeds on the Move Lift-the-Flap Booklet

- Crayons or colored pencils

For Who Will Plant a Tree? *Model*

- Tape
- Glue
- Scissors
- A variety of materials to make seed dispersal models, such as:
  - Play-Doh
  - Pipe cleaners
  - Construction paper
  - Paper towel tubes
  - Fur fabric
  - Craft feathers
  - Yarn
  - Velcro dots
  - Acrylic pom-poms

For STEM Everywhere (per student)

- Balloon
- Toilet paper tube
- About 1 tsp of small, lightweight seeds (such as grass seeds or wildflower seeds) in a zippered plastic bag

Note: The Elaborate phase of this lesson requires an outdoor area, preferably containing tall, unmown grass or weeds.

Student Pages

- Dandelion Observations and Wonderings
- Seed Cards
- What's on My Sock?
- Seeds on the Move
- Who Will Plant a Tree?
- STEM Everywhere

Background for Teachers

A Framework for K–12 Science Education suggests that by the end of grade 2, students should understand that plants have different parts that help them survive, grow, and produce more plants. One of those parts is a seed. Inside each seed is an embryo of a plant that, if conditions are right, will grow into a new plant. Multiple seeds often cannot survive if they are clustered too close to the parent plant because layers of leaves from the parent plant might block the light from reaching the seedlings, or too many roots would compete for water. Thus, it is key for the survival of many plant species that the seeds be moved to other places. The mechanism by which plant seeds are transported to new sites is called *seed dispersal.*

There are many ways that seeds are dispersed. For some seeds, like dandelion and maple seeds, wind simply blows them off the plant and carries them far away. These two seeds have parts that allow them to be easily carried by the wind. Dandelions have white seed heads containing fluffy seeds that catch in the wind and float easily. Maple seeds have winglike structures that allow them to sail on the wind and twist and twirl through the air. Sometimes water moves seeds from place to place. For example, ocean currents can carry coconuts to other pieces of land, where they sprout and grow into new coconut trees. Some plants depend on animals to move their seeds around. Many species of animals carry seeds from place to place without even knowing it. For instance, animals that eat plants will discard the seeds in their droppings. Seeds can also stick to animals' fur or feathers and fall off in another location. In these ways, new plants can grow far away from the tree or plant that produced the fruit.

In this lesson, students explore the crosscutting concept (CCC) of structure and function as they observe various seeds and identify structures that allow the seeds to be moved from place to place, like the hooks on a burdock seed that allow them to stick to fur and feathers, or the *pappus* (fluffy white tuft) of a dandelion seed that allows it to stay aloft. Students use the science and engineering practice (SEP) of developing and using models as they participate in a modeling activity in which they use a sock to mimic animal fur and take a "sock walk" to collect seeds. Next, they use various materials to develop their own model that mimics the function of an animal dispersing seeds. This lesson introduces seed dispersal as an interdependent relationship between plants and animals. This concept will serve as a foundation for the upper elementary grades when students will learn how multiple species are dependent on one another to maintain a healthy ecosystem. When students make their models, they engage in an engineering standard about how designs can be conveyed in drawings and models, which will be expanded upon in grades 3–5 to include researching and testing models.

Learning Progressions

Below are the disciplinary core idea (DCI) grade band endpoints for grades K–2 and 3–5. These are provided to show how student understanding of the DCIs in this lesson will progress in future grade levels.

DCIs	Grades K–2	Grades 3–5
LS2.A: Interdependent Relationships in Ecosystems	• Plants depend on animals for pollination or to move their seeds around.	• Organisms can survive only in environments in which their particular needs are met. A healthy ecosystem is one in which multiple species of different types are each able to meet their needs in a relatively stable web of life.

Continued

DCIs	Grades K–2	Grades 3–5
ETS1.B: Developing Possible Solutions	• Designs can be conveyed through sketches, drawings, or physical models. These representations are useful in communicating ideas for a problem's solutions to other people.	• Research on a problem should be carried out before beginning to design a solution. Testing a solution involves investigating how well it performs under a range of likely conditions..

Source: Willard, T., ed. 2015. *The NSTA quick-reference guide to the* NGSS: *Elementary school.* Arlington, VA: NSTA Press.

engage

Dandelion Observations and Wonderings

Making Connections: Text-to-Self

Show students the cover of *Flip, Float, Fly*, which shows a girl blowing the seeds off a dandelion. *Ask*

? Have you ever seen these fluffy things?

? Where have you seen them? (growing in the ground)

? What do you think they are? (dandelions or dandelion seeds)

? Have you ever made a wish and blown on them? (Answers will vary.)

? What happened to the seeds? (They floated away.)

? What are you wondering about dandelion seeds? (Answers will vary.)

If the season and location are right, take students to an area where they can see dandelions growing, or bring some dandelions into the classroom for them to observe. It is best if you can bring in specimens at different stages of the dandelion life cycle, from the yellow flowers to the fluffy white seed heads. If you are not able to find dandelions, you can use videos and photographs for your observations (see "Websites").

Give students the Dandelion Observation and Wonderings student page. Whether they are observing actual dandelions, watching the videos, or both, have them complete the sketches and the Observations/Wonderings chart. Have students share some of their observations with a partner and then invite them to share with the class. Next, have them share their wonderings with a partner and then invite them to share with the class. *Ask*

? Could you see the seed part of the dandelions you observed? (Have students point out the seeds on their dandelion specimen or in a photograph of a dandelion [see "Websites"]).

? Why do you think dandelion seeds fly like they do? (Answers will vary.)

? What structures or parts of the dandelion seed help it float and fly? (The puffy, fluffy white part connected to the seed allows it to fly.)

explore

Seed Observations

In advance, collect some of the seeds featured in the book *Flip, Float, Fly*. Examples of these seeds are maple, locust, coconut, acorn, burr, and whole fig. (Figs should be cut in half to reveal the seeds.) Give each group of four students a collection of the seeds to observe. Have them use hand lenses to make careful observations of their size, shape, and other characteristics. Having students observe real seeds is preferred, but if you are not able to collect the seeds, you can use the Seed Cards student page.

After the students have observed the seeds, *ask*

? How do you think each of these seeds might be spread to other places? (Have students turn and talk about the characteristics of each seed and share ideas of how these seeds might be moved from place to place.)

? What parts do these seeds have that might help them move to other places? (Answers will vary.)

OBSERVING SEEDS

explain

Flip, Float, Fly Read-Aloud

Connecting to the Common Core
Reading: Informational Text
KEY IDEAS AND DETAILS: 2.1

Determining Importance

Tell students that you are going to read the book *Flip, Float, Fly* to find out how each of the seeds they observed travels from its parent plant. Read the book aloud, stopping before the "Notes" section at the end. As you read, have students signal when they hear about each of the seeds they observed.

After reading, ask students to use evidence from the book to explain how the seeds they observed earlier move from place to place and discuss the parts of the seeds that allow them to do so. For example, the "wing" of a maple seeds allows it to fly far away from its parent tree. Have students toss a maple seed into the air and watch it fly. The open space inside a coconut allows it to float on the water and drift away on the waves. Demonstrate how a coconut floats by placing it in a bowl of water. Burdock seeds have hooks on them that stick to fur, feathers, and even our clothes. Demonstrate how a burdock seed sticks to fabric. *Ask*

? What do you think is the purpose of these seeds being moved away from their parent plant? (Answers will vary.)

Read the "Notes" section on the last page of the book, which explains that many seeds cannot sprout where they form. These seeds depend on animals, wind, and water to move them to another location. Tell students that the process of seeds being moved away from the parent plant is called *dispersal*.

> **CCC: Structure and Function**
> The shape of natural objects are related to their functions.

Seeds on the Move Lift-the-Flap Booklet

 *Writing*

> Connecting to the Common Core
> **Writing**
> RESEARCH TO BUILD KNOWLEDGE: 2.8

Tell students that they are going to have an opportunity to show what they have learned about how seeds are moved. Give each student a copy of the Seeds on the Move student pages. To make a lift-the-flap booklet, have them fold each page on the dotted line and staple the pages. For each page, students should write the name of a seed that travels in that way and then draw the wind, water, or animal helping it move.

elaborate

Who Will Plant a Tree? Read-Aloud

> Connecting to the Common Core
> **Reading: Informational Text**
> KEY IDEAS AND DETAILS: 2.1

 Inferring

Show students the cover of the book *Who Will Plant a Tree?* and ask

? What do you think this book is about? Why? (Answers will vary.)

Encourage students to explain their thinking by referring back to the cover's illustration and title.

Point out the bear, squirrel, and moose on the cover. *Ask*

? Do you think these animals can help to plant a tree? How? (Answers will vary.)

Determining Importance

Ask students to listen for the different ways that animals can help seeds travel from their parent plant to grow in other places as you read the book aloud.

Questioning

After reading, *ask*

? What were some of the ways the animals in the book planted trees? (Seeds stuck to their fur or feathers and then fell off later in a different place, they ate seeds and then pooped or spit them out, and so on.)

? Did these animals know they were planting trees? Did they do it on purpose? (no, except for the people at the end of the book)

Making Connections: Text-to-Text

> Connecting to the Common Core
> **Reading: Informational Text**
> INTEGRATION OF KNOWLEDGE AND IDEAS: 2.9

Ask

? How does this book compare with *Flip, Float, Fly?* (*Flip, Float, Fly* was about wind, water,

and animals moving seeds around. *Who Will Plant a Tree?* was about animals moving seeds around. The books both contained some of the same seeds such as maple, coconut, and fig.)

Sock Walk

Ahead of time, ask each student to bring in an adult-size sock (the fuzzier the better) that will easily fit over one of their shoes. Be sure to have some extra socks for any students who forget to bring them.

Ask

? Do you think animals around our school help to plant trees or other plants without knowing it?

? What kinds of seeds might they collect on their fur?

? How could you use the sock to make a model of an animal's fur?

TAKING A SOCK WALK

SEP: Developing and Using Models
Develop a simple model based on evidence to represent a proposed object or tool.

Tell students that they will be taking a walk outdoors to see if they can collect any seeds. But they won't be using their hands to collect the seeds! Instead, they will be placing a sock over one of their shoes to make a model of an animal's fur-covered leg. As they walk around the school grounds, different kinds of seeds might stick to the socks, just like the seeds in the book stuck to the animals. After the sock walk, they will be examining their socks to see if they collected any seeds.

The best location for a sock walk would be a large unmown area of grass or weeds. Be sure to check for poisonous plants ahead of time. After the walk, have students carefully remove their socks before moving indoors to examine what was collected. Once inside, ask students to use hand lenses

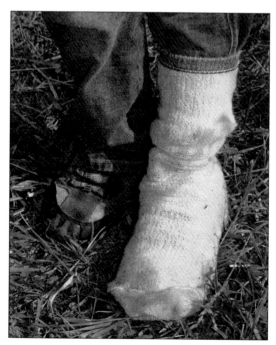

to observe what was collected on their socks. Have students draw and label what they observed on the What's on My Sock? student page.

Note: For an alternative activity, sprinkle an assortment of seeds on students' desks, then have each student put a sock on one hand and do the "sock walk" indoors.

After the sock walk, *ask*

? Which things on your sock do you think are seeds? Why do you think so?

? How could you know for sure? (plant the seeds)

You may want to see if the seeds will sprout by wetting the seed-covered socks with water, placing each in a zippered bag, and keeping them in a warm place for a few weeks.

SAFETY

- Students should wear long socks, long pants, long-sleeve shirts, hats, sunglasses, sunscreen, and safety glasses or goggles.
- Caution students against collecting ticks, mosquitoes, stinging insects, and other potentially hazardous insects.
- Check with the school nurse regarding student medical issues (e.g., allergies to bee stings) and how to deal with them.
- Find out whether outdoor areas have been treated with pesticides, fungicides, or any other toxins and avoid any such areas.
- Caution students against poisonous plants such as poison ivy or poison sumac.
- Bring some form of communication, such as a cell phone or two-way radio, in case of emergencies.
- Inform parents, in writing, of the field trip, any potential hazards, and safety precautions being taken.
- Have students wash their hands with soap and water upon completing the activity.

evaluate

Who Will Plant a Tree? Model

Remind students that the sock they used in the sock walk was a *model* of an animal's furry leg. Tell them that now they are going to be able to come up with their own model that mimics how an animal spreads seeds. Revisit the book *Who Will Plant a Tree?*, asking students to recall the various animals and the ways they move seeds. Provide students with a variety of supplies they can use to make their models. *Ask*

? How could you use these supplies to make a model that shows how a particular animal moves seeds?

? What could you use to represent the seeds?

? What could you use to represent the animal or part of the animal?

? How will you use the model to demonstrate a seed being moved from one place to another?

Give students the opportunity to look through the supplies, touch them, and think about how they might be used. Then invite them to share some of their ideas with partners or groups.

> **SEP: Developing and Using Models**
> Develop a simple model based on evidence to represent a proposed object or tool.

 *Writing*

> Connecting to the Common Core
> **Writing**
> RESEARCH TO BUILD KNOWLEDGE: 2.8

Give students a copy of the *Who Will Plant a Tree?* student page. Have them fill in the sentence "A

_____ planted a _____." with the animal and plant they choose. In the box below, they can write and draw their description of how that animal moves that certain kind of seed. Then they can build their model. Ask students to demonstrate their models for you. Ask guiding questions such as:

? What represents the seeds in your model?

? How does your animal move the seed?

? What parts of the seed make this work?

? What parts of the animal make this work?

? Does the animal know the seed is being moved?

STEM Everywhere

Give students the STEM Everywhere student page as a way to involve their families and extend their learning. They can do the activity with an adult helper and share their results with the class. You will need to send home the following supplies with each student: a balloon (Before using balloons in the classroom, be sure that no one is allergic to latex.), a toilet paper tube, and about a teaspoon of small, lightweight seeds (such as wildflower or grass seeds) in a zippered plastic bag.

Opportunities for Differentiated Instruction

This box lists questions and challenges related to the lesson that students may select to research, investigate, or innovate. Students may also use the questions as examples to help them generate their own questions. These questions can help you move your students from the teacher-directed investigation to engaging in the science and engineering practices in a more student-directed format.

Extra Support

For students who are struggling to meet the lesson objectives, provide a question and guide them in the process of collecting research or helping them design procedures or solutions.

Extensions

For students with high interest or who have already met the lesson objectives, have them choose a question (or pose their own question), conduct their own research, and design their own procedures or solutions.

After selecting one of the questions in the box or formulating their own question, students can individually or collaboratively make predictions, design investigations or surveys to test their predictions, collect evidence, devise explanations, design solutions, or examine related resources. They can communicate their findings through a science notebook, at a poster session or gallery walk, or by producing a media project.

Research

Have students brainstorm researchable questions:

? How far can dandelion seeds travel from their parent plant?

? What kinds of seeds have "wings" other than a maple seed?

? What invention was inspired by the burdock seed?

Continued

Investigate

Have students brainstorm testable questions to be solved through science or math:

? How long does it take for a maple seed to fall from your hand to the ground? How long does it take if you break off the "wing"?

? Can you get maple seeds to sprout?

? Can you get dandelion seeds to sprout?

Innovate

Have students brainstorm problems to be solved through engineering:

? Can you design a model that mimics a maple seed's ability to fly?

? Can you design a model that mimics a dandelion seed's ability to fly?

? Can you design a way to spread grass seeds over a wide area?

Websites

 Photos of Dandelion seeds from PBS
www.pbs.org/wgbh/nova/article/ dandelion-seed-flight

 "The Dandelion" (video) from BBC's *The Private Life of Plants* documentary series
www.youtube.com/ watch?v=slUkyA2cy60

 Time-Lapse Dandelion Flower to Seed Head (video)
www.youtube.com/ watch?v=UQ_QqtXoyQw

More Books to Read

Bodach, V. K. 2016. *Seeds*. Mankato, MN: Capstone Press.
Summary: Simple text and bold, close-up photographs present the seeds of different plants, how they grow, and their uses.

Gibbons, G. 1991. *From seed to plant*. New York: Holiday House.
Summary: This book provides a simple introduction to how plants reproduce. Topics include pollination, seed dispersal, and growth.

Jordan, H. 2015. *How a seed grows*. New York: HarperCollins.
Summary: This updated Let's-Read-and-Find-Out Science book provides a simple introduction to how seeds grow into plants.

Page, R. 2019. *Seeds move!* San Diego, CA: Beach Lane Books.
Summary: Bright, colorful illustrations and simple text show many ways seeds are moved from place to place.

Robbins, K. 2005. *Seeds*. New York: Atheneum Books for Young Readers.
Summary: This book has stunning photographs and straightforward text that explains how seeds grow and how they vary in size, shape, and dispersal patterns.

Stewart, M. 2018. *A seed is the start*. Washington, DC: National Geographic Kids.
Summary: Illustrated with full-color photographs, this nonfiction book shares information on what a seed needs to grow as well as the many fascinating ways that seeds are dispersed.

Weakland, M. 2011. *Seeds go, seeds grow*. Mankato, MN: Capstone Press.
Summary: Simple text and photographs explain the basics of seed parts, how they are produced, and how they can be moved to different places by wind, water, and animals.

Dandelion Observations and Wonderings

Sketch a dandelion and label any parts you know.

Record your observations and wonderings below.

Observations	Wonderings

Seed Cards

Dandelion Seeds

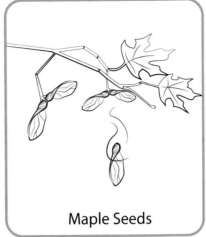

Maple Seeds

Tumbleweed Seeds

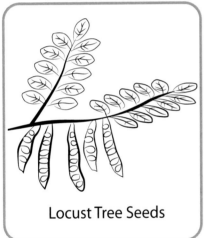

Locust Tree Seeds

Coconut Seeds

Wild Oat Seeds

Fig Seeds

Burdock seeds

Touch-Me-Not Seeds

What's on My Sock?

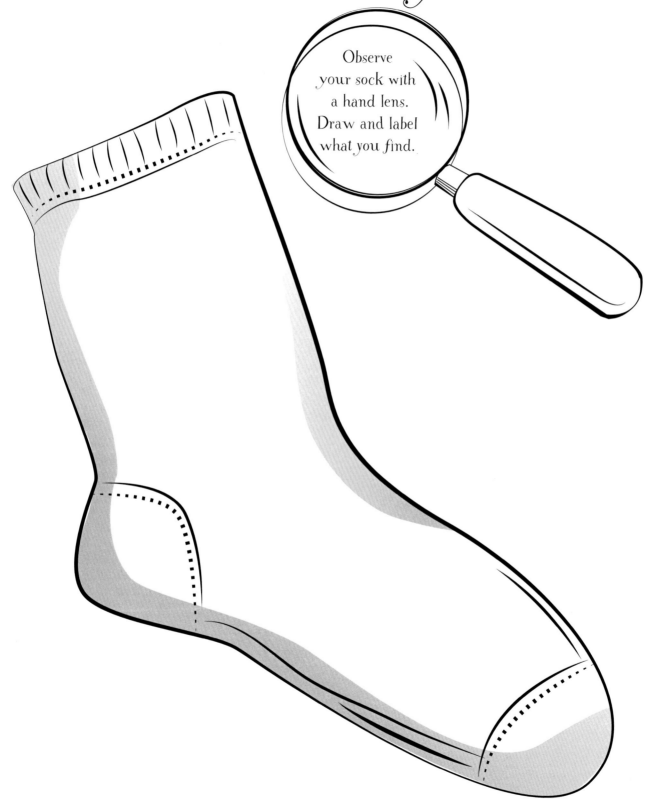

Observe your sock with a hand lens. Draw and label what you find.

National Science Teaching Association

Seeds on the Move

By_____

Water

Wind

Animals

Name: _____

Who Will Plant a Tree?

A _____ planted a _____.

Show in words and pictures how this animal planted the seed.

STEM Everywhere

At school, we have been learning how **many plants depend on wind, water, and animals to move their seeds**. To find out more, ask your learner questions such as:

- What did you learn?
- What was your favorite part of the lesson?
- What are you still wondering?

At home, you can watch a video about some amazing plants that are able to blast their seeds out of the seed pod with explosive force!

 "Seed Dispersal by Explosion" from Smithsonian Channel
www.youtube.com/watch?v=OB0P3mx_IxY

Next, you can make a model of an exploding seedpod. You just need a balloon, a toilet paper tube, tape, scissors, and some seeds.

1. Tie off the neck of a deflated balloon.
2. Cut off the tip of the balloon.
3. Wrap the balloon around one end of a toilet paper tube. Be sure it's snug.
4. Tape the balloon firmly in place.
5. Find a place where you would like to spread the seeds.
6. Sprinkle some of the seeds (not all) into the balloon and pull back the balloon as far as you can. Let go of the back end!
7. How far did your seeds go? Try again with more seeds and watch where they land.
8. Discuss how this model compares to the exploding seedpods in the video.

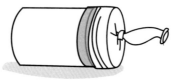

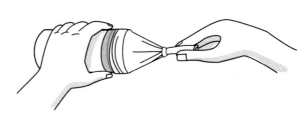

Activity adapted from https://pbskids.org/plumlanding/educators/activities/pdf/SeedBlast_Family_Activity.pdf

National Science Teaching Association